Beauty of
Virginia

Beauty of
Virginia

Text: Parke Shepherd Rouse, Jr.
Concept & Design: Robert D. Shangle

Revised Edition
First Printing October, 1991
Published by LTA Publishing Company
2735 S.E. Raymond Street, Portland, Oregon 97202
Robert D. Shangle, Publisher

"Learn about America in a beautiful way."

This book features the photography of
James Blank
Shangle Photographics

Library of Congress Cataloging-in-Publication Data
Rouse, Parke, 1915-
    Beauty of Virginia / text, Parke Shepherd Rouse, Jr.; concept & design, Robert D.
Shangle.
            p.   cm.
    Revised edition of: Beautiful Virginia / concept and design, Robert D. Shangle;
text, Parke Shepherd Rouse, Jr. 1st ed. c1980.
    ISBN 1-55988-057-0 (hardbound): $19.95. — ISBN 1-55988-056-2 (paperback):
$9.95
    1. Virginia — Description and travel — 1981 — Views. I. Rouse, Parke, 1915-
Beautiful Virginia. II. Title.
F227.R644   1991
917.5504'43 — dc20   91-26979
                                                                                           CIP

Contents

Introduction

It's true that Virginia is the oldest remnant of English-speaking civilization in the New World, but no one should be misled by her age. In spirit, the society planted by John Smith and his 104 fellow settlers at Jamestown in 1607 is youthful and expanding. Lining the shores of Chesapeake Bay at the upper corner of the Sun Belt, Virginia lies "far enough north to *make* a living, yet far enough south to *enjoy* it."

Thanks to her long years of growing corn and tobacco, the Old Dominion has kept her fields and rivers largely unsullied for the nearly 400 years of her life. Though her slowness to industrialize has had its economic drawbacks, Virginia entered the atomic age with the advantages of a clean environment and vast unexploited resources.

One of Virginia's first explorers described her as "a sylvan Venice" because of the interlaced rivers and peninsulas which make up her Atlantic and Chesapeake Bay shoreline. As late as the 1930s, Gertrude Stein observed, after a drive through central Virginia, that the place "looked uninhabited." Virginians took it as a high compliment. They like nature.

Much has changed since the 1930s, but "The Mother of States and Statesmen," as she calls herself, has moved through the centuries without losing herself in a race for wealth or population. Though she occupies a pivotal location on the Atlantic coast, at the northern tip of the Sun Belt, Virginia remains a relaxed, low-pressure state of outdoor living, unspoiled landscapes, and old-fashioned morality. That's how most Virginians seem to want it.

Part of Virginia's taste for the joys of the country and the small town derives from her geography, so beautifully shown in these pages. Waterways and mountains divided Virginia into regions which remained isolated, like the Italian city states of the Renaissance. Not until the 1920s, when highways began to span its rivers and tunnel through its cliffs, was Virginia joined together in one piece.

Even today, the character of Virginia's disparate parts shows in the contrasts between regions. Life is very different on the windswept Eastern Shore from life in the coal-mining fields of Wise County. To understand this proud old state, you should start by looking at her face. Here she is.

P.S.R. Jr.

The Heartland

The heart of historic Virginia is the Peninsula — a 100-mile-finger which projects southward from Richmond to Point Comfort between the James and the York rivers. Chosen by the English settlers in 1607 as the site for their fort — the first permanent English foothold in the New World — it is a low and flat promontory which once belonged to Indians, marsh grass, and pine trees. In the years since 1607, the Peninsula has remained the political center of the colony and Commonwealth. In 1699 the capital was moved to Williamsburg, only seven miles from Jamestown. During the Revolution, in 1780, the seat of government was moved 50 miles westward to Richmond to reduce danger of British attack. There it remains. Today the Peninsula is an important link in the continuous community which stretches from Virginia Beach northward up the Atlantic coast to Boston.

Like all of the Chesapeake basin, the Peninsula is fringed by countless coves, creeks, and rivers. The ragged shoreline has been prized for home and plantation sites since Indian times, and today the land is beyond price. The Chesapeake shore is sandy and gentle. Beaches project from marsh to forest. Once the habitat of waterfowl and Algonquian tribesmen, this frontage increasingly has been taken over for military and industrial use. It is often said to be "worth its weight in gold," and this is hardly an exaggeration. Though January and February bring severe cold and snow, the flora of the Peninsula suggests the tropics. Loblolly pines mark the land as Southern. The Peninsula's southern tip, at Fort Monroe, is fringed with live oaks, the most distinctive of the South's trees. The seasons bring a procession of flowers and bright foliage. Here are dogwood, holly, the spring-flowering Scotch broom, saltbush, and bayberry. Two exotics which especially attract the eye of visitors are crepe myrtle, a lush pink or white shrub which blooms all summer, and magnolia, which has been popular since the day of Edgar Allen Poe for its glossy leafage and huge white blooms. Among the people of the area are many descendants of English settlers who came to Virginia in the 1700s. About a third of the population are black people, whose ancestors began arriving in Virgina in 1619 as workers on the tidal plantations.

Because of the strategic location of the Peninsula, it has been fortified and fought over in the Revolution, the War of 1812, and the Civil War. Descendants of many defenders have remained, with the result that the Peninsula's population is a mixture of "Come-Heres," "Come-Back-Heres," and "Stay-Puts," as they are called. The creation since 1917 of such military bases as Fort Eustis, Langley Field, and Navy and Coast Guard installations at Yorktown has attracted other residents.

The tempo of life on the Peninsula has quickened with the growth of tourism generated by Jamestown, Williamsburg, and Yorktown — the historic triangle wherein British settlement began, reached its pre-Revolutionary crescendo, and was at last ended by George Washington's defeat of the British at Yorktown in 1781.

Though the Peninsula is being urbanized, Virginia is making strong efforts to preserve scenic and historic lands here and elsewhere. Such attractions as Old Point Comfort, the Mariners Museum at Newport News, the Jamestown-Williamsburg-Yorktown triangle, and plantations like Carter's grove on the James provide peaceful contrasts to the busy Interstate Highway 64, which runs down the Peninsula from Richmond to Norfolk. The area suffers from urban sprawl, but it is trying to hold onto its remaining forests, marshes, lakes, and saltwater creeks, where fishing is good from April through November.

Despite all the "Come-Heres," the area has a Southern flavor, especially in summer. Much of life is spent outdoors, and the speech and accents of plantation days are everywhere. Such words as "out" and "about" are still given their peculiar Tidewater pronunciation, inherited from Scottish settlers. The consonant "r" is still dropped by natives, resulting in "heah" for "here" and other Southernisms.

At Jamestown, visitors may still see the tower of the brick church built by the first settlers beginning in 1639, and the rebuilt nave and churchyard with its early tombs. Foundations of early houses have been unearthed and identified, but otherwise Jamestown is made visible through exhibits of its Visitor Center and of the state's Jamestown Festival Park next door. Most exciting of all are the rebuilt ships of the 1607 settlers, *Susan Constant*, *Godspeed*, and *Discovery*, moored at the park on the James River.

Restored since 1926 by the late John D. Rockefeller Jr. and his family, Williamsburg is a living 18th century town encircled by a fringe of shopping centers, hotels, and residential suburbs. In the original town, centering around the mile-long Duke of Gloucester Street, carriages still roll up to the Governor's Palace — the mansion which Virginia's royal governor had to flee in 1755, when Virginians grew angry at his seizure of gunpowder from their public powder magazine.

Down cobbled streets and through dozens of houses and craft shops, the panorama unfolds. Highlights include not only the Governor's Mansion, but also the colonial Capitol, Raleigh Tavern, Bruton Parish Church, and the College of William and Mary, founded in 1695. What makes Williamsburg a peculiar treasure is its role in Revolutionary history. The old town looks much as it did when Washington, Jefferson, Monroe, and Patrick Henry debated there.

Everything is done to keep the 20th century from invading the Historic Area. Cars are ruled out, and dining in old taverns is by candlelight. The town's appeal is enhanced by its re-creation of 18th-century amusements, dress, and craftsmanship. Three 18th-century taverns offer period dining, and costumed craftsmen work at archaic trades.

Only 20 miles from Williamsburg over the Colonial Parkway is Yorktown, on the York River. There the battlefields, on which

Washington and Rochambeau brought the British army to its knees, are preserved by the National Park Service, complete with trenches and battle flags. Of special interest is Surrender Field. To dramatize the Revolution and the Yorktown victory, the Commonwealth of Virginia has built a Victory Center, which contains exhibits, and a museum of Revolutionary history. The Visitor Center further explains the siege, while two historic houses, the Nelson House and the Moore House, offer a view of life as it was in 1871.

A little farther from Williamsburg lie a half-dozen historic plantations along the James, all open to the public. Chief among these are Berkeley, the home of the Benjamin Harrisons of Revolutionary fame; Shirley, the seat of the Hill Carters; Westover, where lived the William Byrds; and Sherwood Forest, to which President and Mrs. John Tyler retired from the White House in 1845.

Like the trans-Peninsula Colonial Parkway, the old river road which winds up the Peninsula from Williamsburg to Richmond is an unforgettable journey. In Jamestown's day, settlers rode horseback through the narrow forest path which led westward up the river to the fall line at Richmond. Along it grew some of the greatest plantation houses in Virginia — several with 10,000 or more acres of tobacco land. Today Route 5, known as the John Tyler Highway, is a pathway which connects Virginia's three capitals. Over this same road thousands of early Virginians migrated westward to the Appalachian regions of Virginia, West Virginia, Kentucky, and beyond. The road also passes the sites of important battles of the Civil War. It was in 1862 that General George B. McClellan led his 100,000 Union men up the Peninsula from Fort Monroe in an effort to take Richmond and to put an end to the Civil War. To his dismay, the Confederates under Robert E. Lee fought him to a standstill in the bloody seven Days' Battles in Charles City and Henrico Counties. Many battlefields are preserved. Along the plantation route are the birthplaces of Presidents William Henry Harrison and John Tyler as well as the site of Thomas Jefferson's wedding. And across the James River to Surry County — a route traversed by Virginia's last ferry boats — are the farming counties of Virginia's Southside.

Richmond is Virginia's banking and medical center as well as its capital. Founded by William Byrd II in 1741, it grew slowly until it became the seat of government in 1780. Jefferson designed the classical Capitol, completed in 1788, after the Maison Carrée in Nismes, France, and Benjamin Harrison and James Monroe served as early governors. The city is notable for its museums, including the 18th century residence of Chief Justice John Marshall, the Poe Shrine honoring one-time resident Edgar Allen Poe, Robert E. Lee's Civil War residence, Jefferson Davis' White House, and the Confederate Museum.

Little of 18th century Richmond remains, but many fine Victorian mansions of wealthy tobacconists survive. The city's location on the high banks of the James is especially appealing, and the collection of heroic statues of Confederate leaders — Lee, Jackson, J.E.B. Stuart, Jefferson Davis, and Matthew Fontaine Maury — makes Monument Avenue one of the most attractive 20th century residential areas in America.

It is a far cry from Jamestown's quiet shores to the Capitol Square of modern Richmond, ringed by skyscrapers. It is the measure of how greatly life has changed since Jamestown's three ships arrived less than 400 years ago at the site only 50 miles down the James.

The Chesapeake

A medieval explorer called it "the noblest bay," and early Spaniards in North America named it "The Bay of the Mother of God." But to the English, who came in 1607 to found a colony at Jamestown, it was "The Bay of Chesupioc" — a vast blue network of waters, verdant peninsulas, and islands teeming with shellfish and waterfowl.

Today we call the region the Chesapeake — a splendid maritime corridor between coastal Virginia and Maryland, biting into the Atlantic coast about midway between Maine and Florida. The big bay is the basis of a distinctive Virginia lifestyle, celebrated in song, story, and the arts. "Chesapeake" is an adjective used to describe everything from sailboats to seafood, architecture, and duck decoys.

The automobile age converted the Chesapeake from treacherous enemy into dependable friend; not until the 1920s and '30s did the bay communities come of age. The growth of roads and bridges has linked thousands of remote peninsulas into a contented whole. The crowning event was Virginia's construction in 1963 of a 17-mile-long bridge-tunnel from Cape Henry, on the Virginia mainland at Norfolk, to Cape Charles on the Eastern Shore. With that, Americans began to discover the attractions of coastal Virginia, whose ragged eastern and western shores still preserve much of the rustic charm of the steamboat age.

This is the area's uniqueness: the close proximity of the industrialized Atlantic corridor to primitive fishing villages and farmlands. Once the traveler crosses the Chesapeake's mouth, from Cape Henry to Cape Charles, he finds himself in another world: sand dunes, sea oats, and fleets of oyster boats cradled in quiet harbors surrounded by marsh grass. It is not far different from the "faire meddowes and goodly tall trees" which settler George Percy described on his arrival in Virginia in 1607.

Indian names dot the Eastern Shore, preserving the memory of Algonquian tribesmen who once sailed the bay in canoes — predecessors of the Chesapeake Bay dugouts still used by oyster-dredgers. A traveler from Portsmouth, Virginia, once wrote from Eastern Shore to a friend at home: "Am in Kiptopeke en route to Pungoteague. On to Wachapreague, Accomack, and Chincoteague." Wrote back his friend, "Where the dickens are you?"

On the map, Chesapeake Bay reaches into Virginia like the ghostly fingers of a mighty hand. Its major Virginia rivers are the James, the York, the Rappahannock, and the Potomac, but there are hundreds of creeks besides. Each estuary has a culture of its own, ranging from the deep-Southern pine-and-peanut empire of the James to the politicized character of the Potomac. Along the half-dozen Tidewater Virginia peninsulas are the historic footprints of great events: of Indian wars, John Smith's explorations, George Washington's Revolutionary maneuvers, and many of the battles of the Civil War. The region is today part of a coastal megalopolis which stretches from Norfolk northward to Boston, embracing the Virginia cities of Chesapeake, Portsmouth, Suffolk, Hampton, Newport News, Williamsburg, Richmond, Alexandria, Arlington, and Fairfax.

Much of Tidewater's charm lies in ancient port towns settled in the 1600s and 1700s by tobacco farmers. The towns sit serenely along the shores of creeks and rivers, their brick and frame houses welcoming homecoming farmers or fishermen at dusk. Along the docks of coastal villages, trawlers and oyster boats ride at dockside, their trailboards bearing the names of wives, mothers, and daughters — *Sue*, *Helen G*, or even *Miss Carrie*. In such towns, ancient vocations like boat-building, crab-picking, and oyster-packing are still practiced by a dwindling few. The once-important tobacco crop has over three centuries moved south of the

James River into Southside Virginia and the Carolinas. Today the Tide-water region has no single dominant interest except its growing role as a region of relaxed living amid industrial cities, factories, universities, and military establishments.

Virginia's tidal peninsulas are linked by a common heritage. It is the heritage of their English antecedents, their inheritance of rural Virginia folkways, and their quiet consciousness of their roots in an ancient region. Though most eastern Virginians today earn their livelihood in urban pursuits, there are many who still find a hard living by tilling the soil or fishing the seas. The men whom the sea attracts are typical of the early Englishmen who settled Virginia: fearless, adventurous, hardy, and usually hard-up. Thus their kind have lived for three centuries, eking out a chancy life from their harvest of blue crabs, bluepoint oysters, clams, scallops, and fish. Once cut off from towns, they still cling to an older lifestyle, and the speech and dress on such Virginia outposts as Tangier and Smith Islands in lower Chesapeake Bay still set their people apart from mainlanders. Sightseers swarm to them each summer by tour boats from Urbanna and Onancock, tramping down narrow streets between clapboard houses, snapping pictures of poke-bonneted women and built-up burial mounds, and gorging themselves on crab cakes and cornbread.

Many know Tidewater Virginia chiefly as the home of its famous denizen, the Chesapeake Bay blue crab, known to science as *calinectes lapidus*. The crab is to Virginia what the lobster is to New England or the shrimp to Louisiana. In such seafood citadels as Nick's in Yorktown, Hurley's in Urbana, or Lou Smith's in Gloucester, crabmeat is glorified in endless ways. Gourmets come from far off, especially during the summer soft crab season.

Despite current conservationism, the bay's long tradition of abundance and free enterprise has made it hard for fisheries inspectors to control the grizzled boatmen who deploy over the bay in search of a living. Few trades have changed so little since colonial times as the waterman's. Except for power-driven dredges to scrape oysters and crabs from the sea

16

Monticello, Thomas Jefferson's Home

Natural Chimneys

Mount Vernon, George Washington's Home

Virginia Beach

Jamestown, The First Settlers Ships Replicas

Shenandoah National Park

Governor's Palace, Williamsburg

Colonial Williamsburg

Jefferson National Forest

Along the Blue Ridge Parkway

Swannanoa Palace and Gardens, Waynesboro

Arlington House from President Kennedy's Grave

William and Mary College Campus

On Thunder Ridge, Jefferson National Forest

Henry House, Manassas Battlefield

Mabry Mill, Blue Ridge Parkway

New Cape Henry Lighthouse, Virginia Beach

Portsmouth Lighthouse Museum

Duke of Gloucester Street, Colonial Williamsburg

Shenandoah National Park

Marine Corps War Memorial, Arlington

Natural Bridge

Norfolk Waterfront

Chatham Manor, Fredericksburg Battlefield National Historic Site

Visitors Center, Fredericksburg Battlefield National Historic Site

Norfolk Skyline Along the Elizabeth River

Shenandoah Valley from Rock Point Overlook

Shenandoah National Park

Memorial Amphitheater at the Tomb of The Unknown Soldier, Arlington

Hampton University

Along the Blue Ridge Parkway

Captain John Smith Memorial, Jamestown

Virginia Beach

Old Point Comfort Lighthouse, Hampton

Yorktown Battlefield

Nelson House, Yorktown

"Gardens By The Sea," Norfolk

Near Virginia Beach

Fort Stedman, Petersburg Battlefield

Assateague Lighthouse

State Capitol Building, Richmond

James Fort at Festival Park, Jamestown

Botanical Gardens, Norfolk

Historic Gadsby's Tavern, Alexandria

Highland Country

University of Virginia

Appomattox Courthouse

Jamestown Monument, Colonial National Historic Park

floor, the fisherman's gear today is much the same as George Washington's, when he sent his slaves into the Potomac at Mount Vernon to net shad and herring to be salted down in kegs for winter use.

Probably the most revolutionary change in Virginia's fisheries in recent decades was wrought by the crab pot. This rectangular metal frame, covered with small-mesh chicken wire, is baited with menhaden and other "trash fish" to attract scavenging crabs through its artful conical openings. Introduced in Chesapeake Bay about 50 years ago, crab pots are now spread so thick over the Chesapeake as to offend boatmen and water-skiers. Their white plastic Clorox bottle buoys, attached by rope to the submerged crab pots, have become a serious hazard in some areas.

As industry and military bases have increasingly rimmed Virginia's shores, wildlife and seafood conservation measures have become necessary. Oil spills and fish kills have further weakened Virginia to ecological problems. As a result, Virginia has increased its supervision over natural resources and waterway use. The Chesapeake Bay Foundation came into being in 1965 to support conservation. To protect marshlands, the Nature Conservancy has bought up six low-lying islands off Virginia's Atlantic shore, while the Commonwealth of Virginia and the United States Park Service have acquired other areas of scenic, historic, and biological interest. At Gloucester Point on the York River, biologists of the Virginia Institute for Marine Science investigate fisheries' problems. Through self-control, the bay's legacy can be preserved for the future.

The preservation of historic values has also gained from the area's increased self-awareness. Since John D. Rockefeller Jr. in 1926 began the restoration of Williamsburg, countless museums have sprung up through this heartland of America. Nearly every Tidewater community has historic buildings — churches, houses, public buildings — which it is preserving. On the peninsula between the James and the York, the historic triangle of Jamestown-Williamsburg-Yorktown has been linked by a 35-mile Colonial Parkway of visual and historic treasures. At Jamestown are also reconstructions of the 1607 square-rigged ships *Susan Constant*, *Godspeed*, and *Discovery* which brought the first Englishmen to their rendezvous with destiny. Elsewhere, old lightships, ferry boats, and other craft are being preserved in museums, or as waterfront curiosities or floating restaurants. Countless other hulls, alas, rot beneath the sun on shoals and beaches, affording picturesque material for artists and photographers.

Since 1607, settlers along Virginia's shores have traded by water. Bay shipping reached its apex about 1900, when steamboats connected river towns with the larger world of Norfolk, Old Point Comfort, Cape Charles, and beyond. Then the automobile began to change all that. Even so, the mystique of "steamboat days" still hangs over the Chesapeake like a haze, reminding today's harried commuters of a gracious past.

The first Chesapeake vessels were simple. The earliest were the Indian dugout canoes of Chief Powhatan's day, copied by Jamestown settlers to provide paddle craft. Slowly the single-log dugout evolved into a sailing craft hewn from three, five, or even seven logs doweled together. This evolved the Chesapeake bugeye, an all-weather sailboat manned by fishermen and shippers down to the present. Other bay craft are the skipjack, still used by some bay watermen to "drudge" oysters; the bay schooner; and the chief glory of Chesapeake shipbuilder, the clipper ship, which grew from the speedy 18th-century Chesapeake Bay pilot boat. Clippers effectively battled British navy ships in the War of 1812 and traded heavily with Caribbean ports for rum and sugar. A handful of each of these vessels still serve as exhibits or pleasure craft. Others are kept in museums at Newport News and in Portsmouth as souvenirs of the age of sail.

Meanwhile, the Chesapeake Bay Bridge-Tunnel continues to introduce millions of Americans each decade to Virginia's water wonders. As a link in the East Coast's north-south Ocean Highway (US 13 and 17), it has introduced endless sightseers to "the noblest bay." Seaward of the tunnel lies the Atlantic, whereon French Admiral de Grasse in 1781 defeated the

British fleet to help end the Revolution. Shoreward a few dozen miles are Jamestown, now an exhibit area, and Yorktown, where the American and French victory of 1781 ended British control of the colonies. The bridge-tunnel is an attraction in itself. Built at a cost of $140 million, it includes two tunnels beneath the bay's two major shipping channels, one leading west to Norfolk, Newport News, and Richmond, and the other north to Washington, D.C. and Baltimore. Four man-made islands of sand and rock support the tunnel entrances. One of them is a small resort in itself, with a restaurant and fishing pier for devotees of striped bass, bluefish, cobia, spot, and trout.

Tidewater Virginia faces the same decisions which confront other favored harbor areas on the Atlantic and Pacific coasts. Can it preserve the natural beauty and resources of its past? Can the seashores and marshes which offer so much to Virginians and visitors survive the growth of population and industry? In traditionalist Virginia, prospects are good that the outdoor lifestyle of the past 375 years will be preserved through this turbulent century. The "sequestered paradise," which novelist James Michener portrayed in his epic *Chesapeake*, won't readily surrender to bulldozers and land developers. Virginia's "land of pleasant living" wants to stay as it is.

The Great Valley

Slanting southwestward from Virginia's northern border is a valley between the Blue Ridge and the Alleghenies. Pioneers called it the Great Valley and wrote glowingly of it. Today we know it as the Valley of Virginia — the cradle of an upland civilization which produced such men as Sam Houston, Cyrus McCormick, Stonewall Jackson, and Woodrow Wilson. The Valley of Virginia offers some of the most picturesque scenery in eastern America. No large cities are here, but dozens of hamlets dot its landscape. Its population has grown slowly. Much of it looks as it did before the automobile revolutionized America.

The valley's crucial years were in the Civil War, when Stonewall Jackson led his Confederates through a whirlwind campaign to drive back the Federals and strike at the District of Columbia. He nearly succeeded before he was mortally wounded at Chancellorsville. His body was brought back to Lexington, adding forever to the lustre of the tough Scotch-Irish valley soldiers.

A look at the map shows the northern valley to be a narrow strand of ten counties, starting with the West Virginia border. Adjacent to it is the Warm Springs Valley, between the Alleghenies and the West Virginia line. Semi-isolated as it is, the Warm Springs Valley is a hunter's and fisherman's paradise, blessed with huge forests and pure mountain streams. Here, in this Switzerland of America, is one of America's great hotels, the Homestead.

Though lowland Virginia was English and African in background, the valley is more dominantly Germanic and Scotch-Irish. First came the

Indians, who called the valley Shenandoah, or "Daughter of the Stars." Then, in the late 1600s came explorers from Tidewater. In 1716 Governor Alexander Spotswood led a cavalcade from Williamsburg to the heights of the Blue Ridge to view the region he claimed for Great Britain, in defiance of France. Despite Spotswood's encouragement of English settlers, the valley was settled chiefly by emigrants from Pennsylvania and Maryland. The first to come were Germanic refugees who came south over the Potomac from Pennsylvania in search of peace and cheap lands. They were Protestants driven from the Saar and the Palatinate by the Catholic King Louis XIV. A few years later a trickle of Ulster Scots, now known as Scotch-Irish, followed and claimed farmlands in the present Frederick and Clarke Counties, at the north end of the valley. Others came later, for the valley lands are rich and they reminded the Ulstermen of their own highlands.

The narrow path down the valley became known as the Great Wagon Road from Philadelphia. As population grew, counties were set up and courthouses built — at Winchester, Harrisonburg, Staunton, and Lexington, among others. The valley today is a blend of English, Scottish, Germanic, and Indian names and legends. Limestone outcroppings provided building blocks for early settlers, and the lime-rich soil afforded rich pasturage for cattle and sheep. Like the Indians before them, the German and Scotch-Irish immigrants followed a well-worn buffalo path which extended through the trough of the valley, following its streams. This wagon road in time became the Valley Pike and today is part of the interstate highway which serves the region.

The valley is at its best in spring, when apple and peach orchards spread their bloom over the hills. In winter the landscape is forbidding, especially during snow. Then the gray fields, black woods, and tiny farmhouses look for all the world like the Rhineland valleys from which many settlers came.

Much of the valley's charm is in the jumble of Germanic and Scotch-Irish styles evident in the farms and houses which lie along the roads. Still evident is the German practice of settling in farm villages so that farmers may share each others' labor and equipment. In early days it also provided confidence and company for those who had not mastered English. Still in use in the valley are tiny stone Presbyterian meeting houses. Other early Anglican, Lutheran, Brethren, and Mennonite churches survive.

Barns are marked with hex signs in some places — a German tradition — and such towns as Winchester, Woodstock, Strasburg, New Market, and Harrisonburg show Germanic building styles. Staunton and Lexington have more of a Scotch-Irish flavor.

The Scotch-Irish had a feistiness which suited them for Indian fighting and for pioneering along the western frontier. Many families settled for a generation or two in the valley and then moved westward into Kentucky or southward into the Carolinas. The forbears of John Calhoun and Andrew Jackson had settled in Virginia before moving south in the 18th century migrations and Indian campaigns.

The agrarian life of the valley is evident. Horse farming and breeding dominate in the northern counties. In green meadows enclosed in split rail or white fences, colts and yearlings play. Horse shows and hunt meets are held frequently in Clarke, Frederick, Warren, and Shenandoah, and the sporting life is evident. Some of America's most famous thoroughbreds are reared in these green meadows.

Dairying is widespread, thanks to the availability of farm labor, and wheat and corn grow lustily in the lowlands along the Shenandoah River. The greening of trees up the mountain slopes each spring signals a new growing season, and rich bottom lands are planted once again. In Page and Rockingham, millions of chicks and turkey poults are hatched each spring, helping to make Harrisonburg the turkey capital of the world.

Winchester is the center of apple growing. Each spring it crowns an Apple Blossom Queen in the presence of princesses and foreign envoys. Mennonites and other Germanic descendants are among the ablest farmers and poultrymen of the region, and their thrifty farms and old-style dress and manners give a certain character to the area.

Front Royal is popular with travelers because of its nearness to Luray Caverns and to the entrance of the Skyline Drive. This mountain-top drive, developed by the National Park Service, carries visitors for more than a hundred miles westward to Waynesboro, where it joins the Blue Ridge Parkway and continues past Roanoke and down into the highlands of western North Carolina. Few roadways anywhere offer so majestic a view of hills and valleys stretching to the distant horizon. Sturdy mountain cabins are silhouetted against the hills. Rushing streams turn ancient mill-wheels. The scenic drive is restricted to pleasure vehicles, and the natural landscape is preserved against changes. An occasional wayside invites the motorist to ponder the view.

By-roads lead from the Skyline Drive and Blue Ridge Parkway to scenes of interest. Near its upper end are such charming horse-country towns as Middleburg, Leesburg, Berryville, and Warrenton. At Winchester is a wealth of Revolutionary and Civil War history, including George Washington's 1760 headquarters and battlefields of Jackson's Valley Campaign. In nearby Frederick County is the pioneer Hopewell Friends Meeting House, while not far away is Belle Grove, a pioneer valley mansion of Germanic origin. At New Market is the Hall of Valor, honoring teenage cadets of Virginia Military Institute who fought there in 1864 to hold back the Union Army. The museum coordinates other Civil War exhibits which dot Jackson's valley trail.

Staunton and Lexington are rich in colleges and schools planted by the Scotch-Irish, whose Presbyterian circuit-riders taught youngsters to read and write so that they might spread the word of God. At Staunton are Maury Baldwin College, Stuart Hall for girls, and several military academies. The birthplace of Woodrow Wilson — the eighth Virginia-born president and the only one to come from the valley — is open to the public here. Nearby Lexington is distinguished as the seat of both Washington and Lee University and Virginia Military Institute. It attracts many visitors because of its Revolutionary and Civil War history. Robert E. Lee is buried in Lee Chapel on the Washington and Lee campus, while Jackson rests with other Confederates in Lexington Cemetery.

Across the Blue Ridge from Staunton is Charlottesville, site of Jefferson's Monticello and of the University of Virginia which he founded. It ranks with Fredericksburg, Alexandria, and the valley towns as among the most attractive in eastern America. Its buildings are chiefly of the post-Revolutionary classical style which Jefferson introduced with his design for Virginia's Capitol at Richmond in the 1780s. The architecture of upcountry Virginia bears Jefferson's strong imprint, unlike earlier Williamsburg and Yorktown.

At Raphine in the valley is the farm where Cyrus McCormick invented the reaper, revolutionizing wheat-growing. Farther west is towering Natural Bridge, a mammoth stone arch visited by millions and long owned by Jefferson. It was once a spa, sought out in summer by health-seekers from the coastal lowlands. Many such valley resorts flourished a century ago, but only Hot Springs and Warm Springs continue today to offer their therapeutic waters in Virginia. Newly popular skiing at Wintergreen in Amherst is great fun.

West of Lexington, the valley narrows as it enters the mountain empire of Southwest Virginia. From Roanoke to the Cumberland Gap, leading into Kentucky, one seeks the rewards of mining and industry, developed to exploit deposits of coal and other minerals which underlie Virginia's western toe. As roads climb, approaching the Cumberland Mountains, the terrain becomes rocky and austere. Fir trees and mountain pines replace the oaks and loblollies of the seaboard. Coal is king here.

Two of Virginia's major cities, Roanoke and Lynchburg, guard the portals to the Southwest. They have become educational centers, nurturing between them nearly a dozen independent and denominational colleges. Extending westward past them, the pioneer trail once travelled by Daniel Boone, John Sevier, Henry Clay, and other emigrants to Kentucky and Tennessee has grown into a four-lane thoroughfare.

South of the James

The James River divides Virginia into today and yesterday. Today is the north side, extending from Newport News to Richmond and thence up the coastal corridor to the District of Columbia. Yesterday is the opposite shore, from Portsmouth to Petersburg, running southwest through the rich black belt of Southside Virginia to Suffolk, Danville, and the North Carolina border.

As you cross the James by ferry from Jamestown to Surry County, you can sense the change. On the south shore life is calmer, slower, and almost totally rural. In this land of farms and forests, the flavor is that of the Deep South. In such counties as Prince George, Isle of Wight, Nansemond, and Sussex, black people make up 70 percent of the population. It is a region of peanut-growing, ham-curing, timbering, and tobacco cultivation. The land is flat and unromantic, but nowhere in America does pulpwood grow faster, peanuts grow bigger, or tobacco grow better flavored.

One of the liveliest towns is Smithfield, where the hams come from. Once it was a drowsy county seat, but today it rumbles to the impact of trucks hauling pigs to its slaughterhouses and cured Smithfield meat to enthusiastic buyers throughout the east. An old town, Smithfield boasts the nation's oldest Protestant church still in use. It is St. Luke's Episcopal, begun in 1632, soon after settlers dared move south of the James to Jamestown into the domain of the pagan Indian tribesmen. Also surviving from that era is the Warren House, built about 1652 on land once owned by Thomas Rolfe, son of Virginia's first tobacco grower, John Rolfe, and his wife, the Indian princess Pocahontas. Nearby is Chippokes, a 19th century plantation which reflects Virginia's tobacco wealth at its height. In the same area is Bacon's Castle, a brick house built beginning in 1655 in the Jacobean style then popular in England.

All along the James River, from Richmond southward to Portsmouth and Chesapeake, small creeks and rivers drain the swamps and forests of Southside. The land grows marshy south of Suffolk, where the great Dismal Swamp is almost impenetrable. Huge cypress trees stand in black swamp waters, their gnarled trunks showing the ravages of centuries. Many of them were there when George Washington, who once owned part of the swamp, explored its vastness. Beautiful? No, but the Great Dismal has the fascination of mystery. Edgar Allen Poe loved it and used it as the locale of his macabre tales. Runaway slaves and other fugitives disappeared into its thick forests, sometimes never to be heard from again. Once it was a haven for bears, wildcats, and rattlesnakes, but hunting and timbering have today reduced its wildlife.

Suffolk is the center of America's peanut industry, buying up the fall harvest of Southside counties and distributing the tasty product around the world. Nearby is Franklin, in the midst of great forests which feed its worldwide lumbering and pulpwood and paper-making operations.

The drama of the Civil War is visible around Petersburg, where Lee's Confederates withstood Grant's siege for more than a year in 1864-65, only to surrender eight days later at nearby Appomattox. Petersburg is a rich tapestry of 18th and 19th century houses and shops, once important as the shipping center for Southside's tobacco lands. Many of its houses and churches were frequented by Lee and his troops. The town is beautifully situated on the Appomattox River, which flows southward to the James. Like Richmond and Lexington, proud old Petersburg likes to recall the exciting years 1861-65, when Virginia was the battleground of America's most tragic war. Here is preserved the Crater battlefield, under which Union soldiers tunnelled to ignite an underground explosion

74

in an effort to dislodge the Confederates. Here is Blandford Church, where countless Civil War soldiers lie buried. At nearby Appomattox is the McLean House, where Grant and Lee met for the surrender of the Army of Northern Virginia. Once dismantled and moved to Chicago for the Columbian Exposition of the 1890s, it was brought back later and replaced as the center of a national park.

South of Petersburg is the tobacco belt, which provides much of the commerce of Farmville, Lynchburg, Danville, and Martinsville. This demanding plant has created a culture of its own, for it requires year-round work. Weathered tobacco barns and curing houses dot the red clay fields of central Virginia, increasing in number as you approach the Carolina line. Tobacco fields are planted carefully, and the plants grow in military formations. Stripped of excess leaves and topped to avert seeding, they are lovingly harvested in late summer to be flue-cured and then carted to market at lively autumn auctions. Once the leaf was marketed at dozens of Virginia and North Carolina hamlets, but today markets are concentrated in major towns. There the tobacco auctioneers' chant enlivens life in the Southside counties from Labor Day almost until Christmas.

The James River was once the chief waterway of tobacco commerce, but today it is the Roanoke River on the Virginia-North Carolina line. Actually, the leaf is no longer shipped on the Roanoke, which has been dammed to provide electric power and recreation for tobacco's heartland between South Boston, Virginia, and Roanoke Rapids, North Carolina. The Buggs Island Dam has given new prosperity to an area once subject to annual devastation by river floods.

Such is Southside, a land of hard-working farm people. Though it lacks the diversity and urbanity of Tidewater and of Northern Virginia, it enjoys what it has inherited from its pre-Civil War plantation past.

The Northern Neck

The region of northern Virginia around the District of Columbia was granted by the British crown in colonial times to the Culpeper and Fairfax families, and it developed differently from the rest of the state. Called "The Northern Neck," it was dominated during the 18th and part of the 19th centuries by the Fairfaxes and their interests. Not until the District of Columbia was cut from northern Virginia and southern Maryland in the 1790s did this area grow rapidly. Alexandria became the leading city of this region with Fredericksburg not far behind. Like Williamsburg and Yorktown, they began as ports but have grown into regional trade centers which serve a growing District of Columbia sprawl.

The Northern Neck contested with the Peninsula for leadership in colonial times, because its tobacco wealth produced a planter society unsurpassed in Virginia. Richard Henry and Lighthorse Harry Lee sprang from the powerful dynasty planted by Thomas Lee at Stratford Hall, in Westmoreland County. Nearby lived George Mason of Gunston Hall, Robert "King" Carter of Corotoman, and James Monroe of Oak Hill. The leadership of the Northern Neck is best symbolized, however, by George Washington. Like Monroe he was born in Westmoreland County, but when he inherited Mount Vernon from his brother, he moved further up the Potomac to Fairfax. These men and their Revolutionary compatriots created a society of large plantations in the Northern Neck, beginning along the Rappahannock and Potomac and spreading in successive generations across the mountains to the west.

The Northern Neck is a land of contrasts. In such suburban

Washington areas as Alexandria and Arlington it is a thickly-populated urban mass, extending in a semi-circle from Woodbridge through Manassas to Leesburg. Beyond this radius it remains an area of farms and forests, though many residents of the Neck commute from 50 to 100 miles to work daily. The peninsula which lies between the Potomac and the Rappahannock — still called the Northern Neck — is the most bucolic of the region. Stratford Hall still gives a lordly tone to the area, preserving the lands and legends of countless Lees for visitors.

Along Chesapeake Bay and the rivers are little fishing and resort towns which offer charming prospects of shore and water. Among these are Kilmarnock, Irvington, and Reedville. At such ports watermen still moor their boats, setting out before daybreak to scour the Chesapeake for fish, crabs, clams, or oysters.

Once important as a port was Fredericksburg, at the fall line of the Rappahannock. An early rival of Richmond and Petersburg among Virginia's fall line cities, its trade dwindled after the river silted up. Even so, Fredericksburg is a refreshing and lively community today. Here is Mary Washington College of the University of Virginia. Here also is the home of Mary Washington, mother of the first president, and the early law office of James Monroe. Among the town's many fine houses is Kenmore, home of Washington's brother-in-law, Fielding Lewis, and his wife Betty. Another is Brompton, now the residence of the college president, and Belmont, a museum of the paintings of artist Gari Melchers, who lived there until his death.

Much of the combat in the years 1861-65 occurred in this region, as armies in blue and in gray fought off enemy blows at Washington and Richmond. Fredericksburg was the scene of two devastating battles, which have left trenches and cemeteries scattered over its face. The National Park Service preserves battlefields and monuments here and at nearby Chancellorsville, where Stonewall Jackson was fatally wounded.

Virginia's most attractive big city is Alexandria, which grew to importance in the 19th century as a Potomac River wheat and tobacco port.

Little commerce comes by water nowadays, but the river is alive with sailboats and other pleasure craft, which cluster in marinas close to the runways of National Airport, between Alexandria and the District of Columbia. Like Charleston and Savannah, the city is a meld of 18th, 19th, and 20th century features. Brick warehouses along its dockside have been converted to shops, boutiques, and restaurants. Old Town Alexandria has become a favored residence of government officials, including Gerald Ford, when he was a congressman and vice president. George Washington had a townhouse in Alexandria, fifteen miles from Mount Vernon. He and Martha dined often there, attended Christ Church, and danced at balls in Gadsby's Tavern, which still dispenses Potomac seafood and Virginia bourbon to guests in its paneled dining rooms.

The town was home to Lighthorse Harry Lee, who fought in the Revolution, and of his son Robert, who was schooled there to enter West Point. Three handsome colonial mansions owned by various Lees are preserved, along with the Carlyle House, where General Edward Braddock had headquarters during the French and Indian Wars and convened the governors of Virginia, New York, Massachusetts, Pennsylvania, and Maryland in 1755 to plan defenses against France.

Like Williamsburg, Old Town Alexandria is a microcosm of the 13th century. Its mellow brick rowhouses serve as homes or shops, and its mansions are museums, libraries, and private residences. The Stabler-Leadbeter shop is one of the nation's oldest apothecaries, and the Friendship Fire Engine Company houses the horsedrawn engine of Washington's day.

Besides nearby Mount Vernon on the Potomac, the suburbs include George Mason's handsome house, Gunston Hall, and Woodlawn, on a site which George Washington gave his adopted daughter, Nelly Parke Custis, when she married his nephew, Lawrence Lewis. These and many of Alexandria's treasured sites are open to the public.

In the rolling fields of Loudoun, Fauquier, Clarke, Fairfax, and other northern Virginia counties, visitors see an impressive array of 18th and 19th century country estates nestled on hillsides where livestock graze. They are the houses of millionaires, statesmen, and old Virginia families who find life interestingly varied here, close to the bubbling political cauldron in Washington. Several of the nation's most exclusive fox-hunting associations meet in northern Virginia, the hunters decked out in red or black coats and their spotted hounds in full cry as they race across fields and fences in pursuit of the fox.

The scene is far different from that of the Eastern Shore, or from the Southside pinelands, or from the Rockingham Mennonite farms. Yet each is equally a part of this state of oceanfront and mountains, of quiet inland farms and noisy tobacco auctions. Despite her yearning for a golden mean, Virginia is a state of geographic and visual extremes.